ι

Duncan McLean

from original texts by

Pol Heyvaert and Dimitri Verhulst

Methuen Drama

Published by Methuen Drama, 2007

1 3 5 7 9 10 8 6 4 2

Methuen Drama
A & C Black Publishers Limited
38 Soho Square
London W1D 3HB
www.acblack.com

ISBN: 978 0 7136 8737 8

A CIP catalogue record for this book
is available from the British Library

Typeset by Country Setting, Kingsdown, Kent
Printed in the UK by CPI Bookmarque, Croydon, CR0 4TD

Caution

This book is produced using paper that is made from wood grown
in managed, sustainable forests. It is natural, renewable and recyclable.
The logging and manufacturing processes conform to the environmental
regulations of the country of origin.

The National Theatre of Scotland,
Victoria and Tramway
present

Aalst

in a new version by
Duncan McLean

Aalst

Cast

Cathy Delaney	Kate Dickie
Michael Delaney	David McKay
Voice	Gary Lewis
Director and Designer	Pol Heyvaert
Assistant Director	David Overend
Sound Engineer	Matthew Padden
Stage Manager	Paul Claydon

Aalst was first produced by Victoria in 2005 and has since toured extensively in Europe and Canada.

This new Scottish version was adapted by Duncan McLean from original texts by Pol Heyvaert and Dimitri Verhulst, and directed by its original creator Pol Heyvaert.

This version was first performed at Tramway, Glasgow, on Wednesday 21st March 2007.

Tour Schedule 2007

Tramway, Glasgow
21st – 31st March

Macrobert Arts Centre, Stirling
3rd – 4th April

North Edinburgh Arts Centre
5th April

Eastgate Theatre & Arts Centre, Peebles
7th April

Brunton Theatre, Musselburgh
10th April

Paisley Arts Centre
14th April

Soho Theatre, London
17th – 28th April

Warwick Arts Centre, Coventry
8th – 10th May

Customs House, South Shields
12th May

Traverse Theatre, Edinburgh
15th – 19th May

THE COMPANY

Kate Dickie
(Cathy Delaney)

Kate trained at RSAMD. Her theatre work includes: *Trojan Women, Electra, Bonjour Tristesse* (Theatre Cryptic), *Boiling A Frog* (7:84), *Running Girl, Blooded* (Boilerhouse), *Lament, Mainstream, Timeless* (Suspect Culture), *AD* (Raindog), *Home* (Lookout Theatre Company), *JG Ballard Project – Phase 1* (Stuart Laing and Donna Rutherford Productions), *Let Her Body Become a Living Letter* (Crush Theatre Company), *Blood and Water, The Merchant of Venice* (The Arches Theatre Company).

TV work includes: *Still Game 3, Taggart* (SMG/STV), The Vice (Carlton), *Tinseltown I and II* (Raindog/Indigo Productions), *Rab C Nesbitt, Isabelle* (The Comedy Unit).

Film work includes: *Red Road* (Sigma/Zentropa) for which she was awarded Best Actress, British Independent Film Awards; Prix Interpretation Décernée, Festival Nouveau Cinema, Montreal; Best Actress, BAFTA (Scotland), *The Harvest* (55 Degrees), *The Marriage Counsellor* (Emergency Productions*), Room for the Night* (Oxygen Films).

Radio work includes: *Hop, Skip and Jump* (BBC Radio Scotland).

Pol Heyvaert
(Director and Designer)

Pol Heyvaert has a long-standing relationship with Victoria. He was the Set Designer for several of their productions including: *Moeder en Kind* (1994), *Bernadetje* (1997), *Dansé Donsé Dan Dan* (1995), *Auri Sacra Fames* (1997), *Limbus Patrum* (2000); the three dance shows Latrinité, *Wayn Storm* and *Carmen Story, Mise-en-Traub V* (2001), and two Wayn Traub productions *Snack Bar Tragedy* (2002) and *White Star* (2004).

Pol also founded the Kung Fu collective together with Felix van Groeningen, where he directed *Best Of* and *Discothèque*. He has also worked as Set Designer for Les Ballets C de la B, notably for Alain Platel's *Lets Op Bach* (1998), and for Nieuwpoort-theater with *De 10des* (1994), *Napels* (1996), *Radio Carmen* (1996) and *Flippers* (1996). In 2001, he collaborated with Felix van Groeningen again on the Kung Fu short film *Bonjour Maman* and as a Production Designer for the feature film *Steve + Sky. Aalst* is the first major theatre production Pol has directed, and since the original production, he has also made a documentary on the same subject. In 2006, Pol also collaborated on the direction and set design of the latest Victoria production, *Nightshade*, which toured Europe extensively in 2006-07.

Gary Lewis
(Voice)

Theatre work includes: *The Grapes of Wrath* (7:84), *One Flew Over The Cuckoo's Nest, Ecstasy* and *Wasted* (Raindog), *The Birthday Party* (Arches Theatre Company), *Snow White* (Tron Theatre Company), *10 Days In May* (Workers' City), Freddy Anderson's *Krassivy: The Story of John MacLean* and *Rafferty's Cafe* by Julia Darling.

TV work includes: *Rehab, Prime Suspect 7, Super Volcano, Rebus, Gunpowder Treason and Plot, Boudicca* and *The Many Trials of One Jane Doe*.

Film work includes: *Yes, Gangs of New York, Solid Air, One Life Stand, Billy Elliot, Orphans, Carla's Song, My Name Is Joe, Ae Fond Kiss, Yasmin, True North, The Escapist, Pure, Niceland, Scaggerak, Joyeux Noël, Eragon, The Rocket Post, Blessed* and Samuel Beckett's *What? Where?*

Radio work includes: *Germinal, Falco, A Breath of Air, Breaking Bread* and James Kelman's *The Art of the Big Bass Drum* (BBC Radio).

Documentary includes: *Dungavel, Monster of the Glen* (Camcorder Guerillas).

David McKay
(Michael Delaney)

David trained at Glasgow Arts Centre. His theatre work includes: *The Tempest, Salvation* (Tron Theatre), *Wishing Tree, Damaged Goods,* (Wiseguise*)* *One, Two, Hey* (Traverse Theatre), *Conquest of the South Pole* (Raindog), *Of Mice and Men* (Brunton Theatre), *Shining Souls, Hansel and Gretel, The Lion the Witch and the Wardrobe,* (Citizens' Theatre), *The Game's a Bogie* (7:84), *Ten Days in May, Pals* (Cumbernauld Theatre), *Aladdin* (Pavilion Theatre*)*, *Smugglers, Tellyitis, An Me Wi A Bad Leg Tae, When Hair Was Long and Time Was Short* (Borderline), *The Celtic Story, Harmony Row* (Wildcat), *The Big Move* (Skint Knees Theatre), *Wuthering Heights* (Birds of Paradise) *Hair of the Dog* (Dependency Culture).

TV work includes: *Shoe Box Zoo, Looking After Jo-Jo, Para Handy, Down Among the Big Boys, Justice Game, Down Where the Buffalo Go, Workhorses* (BBC), *Rab C Nesbitt* (BBC Scotland), *Stookie, Taggart,* (STV).

Film work includes: *Ae Fond Kiss* (Sixteen Films Ltd), *Once Upon A Time in the Midlands* (Midland Films Ltd*)*, *My Name is Joe* (Parallax), *Les Misérables* (Les Misérables Prods), *Braveheart* (Braveheart Productions*)*, *Initiation* (Wiseguy Ltd), *Close* (STV), *Nightlife* (BBC Scotland),

Joyride (Sidewalk Prods/BFI), *The Girl in the Picture* (Antonine Productions), *As Far As You've Come* (La Belle Allée Productions).

As a Director: *Tinsel Town*, *My Barmy Aunt Boomerang*, *The Basil Brush Show* (BBC), *My Parents are Aliens*, (Yorkshire TV), *Cracked*, *High Times* (SMG) He also wrote and directed three films, *Caesar*, *To A Mouse* and *Final Warning* (Hampden Films, Ideal World, SMG).

Duncan McLean
(Writer)

Duncan was born in Aberdeenshire in 1964, and has lived in Orkney since 1992. While based in Edinburgh in the 1980s, he started writing songs, stand-up routines and plays for the Merry Mac Fun Co, a street theatre and comedy act with agit-prop tendencies. The Merry Macs won various awards, and were twice nominated for the Perrier. They were able to perform in a great range of venues from community halls in Shetland to West End theatres in London, and from unemployed workers' centres in Rutherglen to the Wogan show on BBC1.

In 1992 he published his first book, a collection of short stories called *Bucket of Tongues*, and since then has published several more including two novels and a first collection of plays, imaginatively entitled

Plays: One. Around this time he also set up and ran the Clocktower Press, a small but influential publishing house, which helped bring a new generation of Scottish writers to wider attention.

In recent years he has divided his time between writing, music and selling wine and whisky in his wife's family business in Orkney. In 2006 he won the prestigious trade award, UK Restaurant Wine Supplier of the Year. In spring 2007 he returned to writing as his full time occupation (more or less) for the first time since 1997.

David Overend
(Assistant Director)

David studied Theatre and Dramaturgy at Glasgow University. He was Literary Assistant at the Traverse Theatre last year and is now training as a director at RADA. Directing credits include *Petra* by David Greig (Measureless Liars & GilmorehillG12), *The Open Couple* by Dario Fo and *The Tempest* (Measureless Liars). Co-directing credits with James Oakley include *The Gyntish Self* by Robert Drummond, Ewen Glass and Alan Gilmour, and *Afraid of the Dark?*, a devised piece (Measureless Liars). He has also assistant directed *Cathy & Heathcliff*, William Gaskill's adaptation of *Wuthering Heights* at RADA.

[NATIONAL THEATRE OF SCOTLAND]

The National Theatre of Scotland launched to the public on 25th February 2006 with its unique and defining opening event *Home*, which saw ten directors create ten pieces of work based on the theme of 'home' in ten different locations around the country. Since this flagship event, the National Theatre of Scotland and the audience response to it have re-invigorated my belief in the power of theatre to connect, to transform, to challenge and to transcend.

The National Theatre of Scotland has no building. Instead, we take theatre all over Scotland and beyond, working with existing venues and companies and, indeed, new spaces and companies, to tour and create theatre of the highest quality. Since we have no bricks-and mortar institutionalism to counter, all our money and energy is spent on creating our work. Our theatre really is without walls. It takes place in the great buildings of Scotland, but also in site-specific locations, community halls and drill halls, car parks and forests.

To date over 130,000 people have seen or participated in our work. We have produced 28 pieces of work in 62 locations from the Shetlands to Dumfries, and from Belfast to London. In our inaugural year, we took both the Edinburgh International Festival and the Fringe by storm, winning a clutch of awards including two Herald Angels, a South Bank Show Theatre Award, a Scotsman Fringe First, a Best Theatre Writing Award from The List and a Stage Award for Best Ensemble. In 2007/8, the international stage beckons, with tours to the USA and Australasia currently being finalised.

This season, along with *Aalst*, we will embark on an ambitious UK tour of the highly acclaimed *The Wonderful World of Dissocia*, written and directed by Anthony Neilson. The site-specific *Black Watch* will leave its Edinburgh home and tour all over Scotland, before a London residency as part of the Barbican's bite 07 Festival and a US tour. At the same time, *Tutti Frutti* will play in Glasgow, Edinburgh and Blackpool and *Futurology* (a co-production with Glasgow's Suspect Culture) will tour conference centres from Aberdeen to Brighton.

Meanwhile, our Young Company will be working with creative director Mark Murphy on *The Recovery Position* – a promenade piece designed specifically for their home at Platform in

Easterhouse, Glasgow. Our Learn department will be busy with their Transform and Connecting Communities events all over Scotland and will host their second youth theatre festival in Stirling. To mark the Highland Year of Culture, *Project Macbeth* will return for a special production in Elgin Cathedral, and summer will see the world premiere of *Venus as a Boy*, an NTS Workshop co-production with Burnt Goods based on Luke Sutherland's extraordinary novel.

Scottish theatre has always been for the people, led by great performances, great stories or great playwrights. The National Theatre of Scotland exists to build a new generation of theatre-goers as well as reinvigorating the existing ones; to create theatre on a national and international scale that is contemporary, confident and forward-looking; to bring together brilliant artists, designers, composers, choreographers and playwrights; and to exceed expectations of what and where theatre can be.

Vicky Featherstone, Artistic Director

*For more information about
the National Theatre of Scotland, visit*
www.nationaltheatrescotland.com
or call +44 (0) 141 221 0970

Our Co-Producers on *Aalst*

VICTORIA

Victoria always puts creativity at the heart of everything it does, developing new ideas, finding new forms of theatre, and reacting to things that happen, to reality. Our main motivations are the search for the unconventional and finding a different approach to theatre. Most of the time, this involves focusing on creating a new definition of what already exists and repeating it in a different context.

This remake of *Aalst*, in partnership with the National Theatre of Scotland and Tramway, is a perfect example of this process. By transferring the production to new writers, new actors, new theatres and new countries, the production has been strengthened by a fresh approach, enriched by the different experience of the actors, a different way of making theatre and the differences between countries. It is fascinating for us to connect a director with actors from another country. This connection works both ways and everyone involved develops as an artist in the process.

TRAMWAY

Tramway is one of the leading contemporary visual and performing arts venues in Europe. Audiences, visitors, artists, performers and producers seek out Tramway's unique spaces as a place to create and engage, challenge and question.

This co-production signifies the high ambition of both Tramway and the National Theatre of Scotland to experiment and explore new avenues of creativity. We hope that our combined commitment to creating a platform for international work will serve as a bridge for both incoming and, most importantly, outgoing work created here in Scotland.

Aalst is a first for both Tramway and the National Theatre of Scotland. A production based on real events, born in Europe, re-worked, re-shaped and re-imagined for a Scottish audience. *Aalst* offers the opportunity for Victoria and their work to be seen in theatres across the UK. The prospect is exciting in its beauty and simplicity, yet at its core quite daring and in no small way brave.

[NATIONAL THEATRE OF SCOTLAND]

BOARD AND STAFF

Introduction

I have written about a fair number of unpleasant and even appalling characters in my stories and plays, but nothing prepared me for the months I've spent in the company of Michael and Cathy Delaney. The background against which their terrible actions are played out is low key and familiar to the point of mundanity. This makes it hard to establish a protective distance between us and them. And the stark, unflinching, direct-address form of the play ensures that any distancing is impossible. That must be one of the reasons why *Aalst*, in performance, has such fearful power: we are in a position of unshielded intimacy with these two we'd rather run from. As we sit in our seats, staring at Michael and Cathy, they sit in their seats a few feet away, staring right back at us.

It was John Tiffany at the National Theatre of Scotland who asked me last summer if I'd be interested in writing an English version of *Aalst*, a play that had recently been 'big in Belgium'. I've never asked him why he chose me, but I can think of a couple of likely reasons. Firstly, because in earlier plays like *Rug Comes to Shuv* and novels like *Bunker Man* I'd been willing to explore the lives of people who felt the world was treating them cruelly, and who responded by turning back on the world in demented rage – a rage that was often vented on their nearest and dearest, and sometimes involved destruction and violence. Secondly, and more importantly, I think John would have been remembering my fascination with direct address in the theatre, which I'd experimented with in both short and full-length plays, as well as in stand-up comedy and street performance. What I value above all else in theatre is its immediacy, the directness with which it can communicate: the unmediated transfer of ideas, emotions and stories from one person – the actor – to another – the audience member.

The original Flemish script was sent to me, and I made what I could of it – not much! The literal English translation that followed helped a little, but I was still baffled by a lot of the play. I had no context within which to situate the characters, I had no clear idea of who or what The Voice was; I had no understanding of the extent to which the play was based on real-life events – and whether or not it mattered. And I knew nothing at all about Aalst: it's not a town that has inspired copious pages of colourful tribute on the Web. Luckily, all that would be remedied by four intensive days in Victoria's theatre in Ghent, working with *Aalst*'s writer/director, Pol Heyvaert.

Aalst turned out to be a large town just off the motorway, about halfway between Brussels and Ghent. The site of Belgium's earliest mass industries (and earliest labour movements), by the end of the twentieth century it was largely post-industrial, except for a huge sugar refinery that occupied several blocks in the middle of the town and puffed out pungent, sickly clouds across the rooftops. It reminded me of a more depressing version of Kirkcaldy or Falkirk.

The real story on which *Aalst* is based took place almost entirely in this grey and run-down environment. Although some details – including all personal names – have been changed, I found that Pol had been remarkably faithful to the real events. He had also been very true to the actual words of the real people. For, in an unprecedented move in that country, Belgian TV had been given access to the courtroom to make a documentary about the trial.

Working on the play in Ghent involved a straightforward routine: Pol and I would sit across a table, each with the English literal, and the Flemish original. And so line by line, word by word, we went through the play, starting to create a third version on the blank pad in front of us. Sometimes the work flowed quickly; other times it was very slow, with the two of us spending an hour discussing the differences between, say, the English words 'kill', 'murder' and 'slaughter' – and then their Flemish equivalents. Occasionally we would take a break and walk along Ghent's charming and picturesque canals, perhaps to look in on the courtroom where the real-life drama unfolded, or to visit the amazing Dr Guislain museum, a nineteenth-century psychiatric hospital that now houses one of Europe's greatest collections of 'outsider art'.

The longer I worked on *Aalst*, the more I came to appreciate how carefully constructed it was, both syllable by syllable – through shifting tones, insistent repetitions and revealing stumbles – and on a larger structural scale: as themes weave in and out, stories are told and retold with new emphases, objects appear first as innocent incidentals, then reappear as deadly weapons. Despite its roots in court transcriptions, and despite the shocking and horrible events it relates, *Aalst* is certainly no brutish rant: Pol's script is subtle, tightly worked and honed over many rewritings and rehearsals. And most remarkably, it doesn't seem like hard work for a second: it seems fresh, direct and immediate, as if we were the first audience ever to hear these horrific tales.

I mentioned above my creating a third version of *Aalst*, starting back in the Victoria office in Ghent. Actually that's not really true: what Pol and I have tried to do for NTS is not to create a new version, but to recreate the original version in English. Nothing has been added (I wasn't allowed to move the setting to Scotland and rename the play *The Lang Toun*) and we have also tried hard not to leave anything out. Inevitably there will be things a non-Belgian audience doesn't immediately 'get'. The Voice, for instance: his words are based on those of the judge in the original trial, and a Belgian audience would no doubt recognise their tone and content as such. To a non-Belgian audience, the latitude the judge has to interrogate and give his views on the couple in the dock might be surprising. But it was there in the Ghent courtroom, and it is there in *Aalst* – and it certainly makes good theatre.

Finally, and indispensably in making good theatre, I should mention the three actors – Gary Lewis, Kate Dickie and David McKay – whom it has been my pleasure to work with in rehearsals in Glasgow. The commitment they showed to immersing themselves in what was a very painful and punishing text was admirable. I'm not embarrassed to say that translating *Aalst* left me on several occasions in tears of horror and sorrow. The actors have the unenviable task of inhabiting the moral universe of Michael and Cathy through many days of rehearsal and many nights of performance. I don't know how they can do it – but they do it brilliantly.

I will finish by recounting a moment from the second or third day of our rehearsals. Not for the first time (nor the last), we were discussing what right we had to make theatre out of the fragments of real lives, and of the real suffering of the children. How dared we write about these things and act them out, even sell tickets for the spectacle? After the real-life Delaneys had been hauled before the court, in a way that, despite the best of intentions, seemed sadly inadequate in terms of either understanding what led them to do what they did, or in memorialising their victims, what right had we to drag it out into the open all over again in a fictionalised form – and in a fiction that is no doubt full of its own sad inadequacies?

But then, as Gary Lewis said, maybe art can help us understand people in a way a court of law can't. And maybe art has a responsibility to try and understand things we can't get at any other way – that's what it's for. I think Gary is right, and in that light I commend Pol Heyvaert's *Aalst* to you.

Duncan McLean
Orkney, February 2007

Aalst

Characters

Voice
Cathy
Michael

Cathy Delaney, I'm led to believe you used to like crosswords?

CATHY

Yes.

Well, what we're going to try and do here is solve the crossword puzzle of your life.

CATHY

Yes.

Michael Delaney, your parents were advanced in years at the time of your birth. They were fifty-five and fifty-six years old respectively, I see. Do you remember when your father deceased?

MICHAEL

In 1972.

In 1974. There were other children in the family. How many were you?

MICHAEL

Six of us. One brother and five sisters.

One brother and *four* sisters, plus yourself; that makes six, right? You spent some time in a young offenders' institution, Mr Delaney. Why was that?

MICHAEL

Because I was convicted of robbery. With my brother.

Convicted of a robbery, with your brother.

MICHAEL

Yes, *robberies*.

***Robberies*. Do you recall how many you committed?**

MICHAEL

About thirty.

**About thirty, you say? Let's not get carried away. I
counted twenty-one, to be precise. When you were at
that institution, Mr Delaney, did you stay put?**

MICHAEL

Yes.

**I think not, Mr Delaney: you absconded. Why was
that?**

MICHAEL

I did run away. I was fed up of that place. Banged up every
weekend, couldn't go home.

**You weren't allowed out at weekends. You thought you
knew better than that?**

MICHAEL

Yes . . . no, sir.

You went to Holland then. Where exactly in Holland?

MICHAEL

The Dam. Amsterdam.

**You were a youth of fourteen or fifteen. And you
travelled with an older friend, aged twenty-two?**

MICHAEL

That's right. That was my pal Stevie.

And then what did you do?

MICHAEL

Then I went to France.

Where in France?

MICHAEL

Paris, I think.

**So you had a liking for the big cities . . . Paris and
Amsterdam. How much money did you have with you?**

MICHAEL

About three thousand.

You mentioned six or seven thousand.

MICHAEL

I don't remember. It was Stevie's.

What happened in Paris?

MICHAEL

We turned ourselves in at the Embassy.

Why?

MICHAEL

Because we'd run out of money.

So you got through two or three thousand in a month? You *were* enjoying yourselves!

MICHAEL

Yes.

Cathy Delaney, you were placed in a children's home. By whom?

CATHY

I was placed in a children's home by my mother.

You were placed in a children's home by your mother. Why were you placed in a children's home by your mother?

CATHY

I don't know why I was sent there. No one ever told me why, never.

It was never talked about. Because you said – and it touched me – in the investigation, you said you had been hidden away, in a children's home in the country. You thought they wanted rid of you? Was that it?

CATHY

Yes.

Were you at that time still in touch with your father?

CATHY

Yes, I used to go home at weekends.

Your father met someone else then, didn't he?

CATHY

Yes . . . but I can't quite remember her name right now.

Yes . . . it was Margaret Simmons. And did you continue to visit your father while he was living with Mrs Simmons?

CATHY

Yes, but she would never let me stay there. She always wanted me out of the way.

She wanted you out of the way.

CATHY

She used to slip me money to stay in hotels. I was often sent to reside with friends and for the Christmas holidays.

What did your father think of that?

CATHY

He didn't know what was happening. He thought it was me, running away.

How did your father treat you?

Cathy mumbles.

You had to perform certain acts for him. Were they *sexual* acts?

CATHY

Yes.

And you never talked about it to anyone?

CATHY

No.

And at this time . . . he wanted you to do your best at school.

CATHY

Yes.

What were you studying?

CATHY

Textiles . . . at technical college. Then hairdressing.

But you had started hoping for an office job, hadn't you?

CATHY

That's right, an office job.

And then you gradually changed your courses, settling for something easier each time?

CATHY

Yes.

Then your father met another woman. Making her his fourth wife?

CATHY

Yes, Paula. But I got on better with her.

Was your father working at the time?

CATHY

He was on disability.

And those acts you mentioned, that your father performed on you, those acts you had to do for him, did they stop at a particular moment?

CATHY

Yes, when I got together with Michael.

Michael Delaney, the first instance of violence towards Mrs Delaney dates back to 1993, when you had only known her for two weeks. You beat up your new girlfriend. Tell me: what was that all about?

MICHAEL

I didn't beat her up! All I did was give her a slap.

Only a slap.

MICHAEL

. . . Yes. And . . . I was wearing a ring. I know, it's not on, you don't hit women. But there are lassies who take advantage of that.

They take advantage.

MICHAEL

They take advantage of the fact that they're women. But I know: it's just not on. So . . . I didn't hit her, I slapped her. Because she's a woman. If she'd been a guy, I would have given her a right good beating, but as it is, I just . . . slapped her. Like I said, I was wearing a ring, so it would've been a lot worse if I'd hit her. I could've punched, I could've slapped . . . I let her off lightly, because I didn't want to hurt her. If she hadn't been wearing glasses, she would've been fine. It was those glasses, really, that hurt her! She was hurt so hard because I was wearing a ring and she was wearing glasses. That's it. But I didn't hit her.

Did you ever try to hold down a job, Mr Delaney?

MICHAEL

No, but I did a lot of work.

How could you go out moonlighting, yet not hold down a proper job?

MICHAEL

Because . . . of the debt collectors.

You were in debt?

MICHAEL

Yes, sir.

How did you get into debt?

MICHAEL

By getting stuff on credit and never paying.

And you borrowed money too?

MICHAEL

Yes.

CATHY

We bought a whole load of stuff from catalogues, that's what we did. You pay in instalments. But we never paid.

How much did you receive in social security benefits?

CATHY

About seven hundred and fifty.

In a month, how much could you earn, Mr Delaney?

MICHAEL

About seven hundred and fifty.

Larger sums have been mentioned, Mrs Delaney. How much was it really?

CATHY

Sometimes fifteen hundred, sometimes . . . you know . . . depending how much work.

Well, fifteen hundred and seven-fifty, that makes two thousand two hundred and fifty per month . . . Surely that was enough to pay off what you bought?

CATHY

Yes.

And why were the debts *not* paid off?

CATHY

Probably we didn't feel like it, I suppose. I don't know.

When you went into hospital to have your daughter, how soon after Ellie's birth did you go home?

CATHY

The same day I was home.

The same day?

CATHY

I wanted to be with Michael.

It wasn't because of hospital fees?

CATHY

No, because we'd only have to have paid later.

You went frequently to social security?

CATHY AND MICHAEL

Yes.

Why's that?

CATHY

We applied for emergency support.

Applied for emergency support.

CATHY

Yes.

With seven hundred and fifty in benefits per month and another fifteen hundred from moonlighting, applying for emergency support. First you deny having financial problems and then you tell us you did have financial problems. Can you explain that?

CATHY

That is not the reason we did it, it wasn't because of financial problems, that's the reason.

Yes. So you weren't forced to do it due to financial problems?

CATHY

No.

MICHAEL

I took her out of the cot and laid her on the mattress beside my wife, and then I pushed her head down into the mattress for a few seconds, to suffocate her.

To suffocate her?

MICHAEL

I couldn't do it. I let her go straight away. I told my wife: here, you finish it.

And what did she do?

MICHAEL

She took that pillow and put it over her, and she lay on top of it.

CATHY

I don't remember that.

Why don't you remember that?

CATHY

He slapped me in the face, burnt me with cigarettes, with a razor he . . . carved my legs up. And as well, in my pubic hair, he wrote the letter M.

Is that the case, Mr Delaney?

MICHAEL

Yes.

Immediately after the events, Mrs Delaney . . .

CATHY

Yes.

. . . you told the officers who took your statement: 'On Thursday night I held my wee girl, Ellie, like this, to my chest, and kept her there until I was sure she was no longer alive.'

CATHY

No, I didn't pick her up, and I didn't press her to my chest. That I don't know.

Why are you espousing this vagueness regarding the death of Ellie?

CATHY

It's the truth.

And what did you do then?

MICHAEL

I stabbed those scissors into his back.

You stabbed those scissors into his back. What did you do, Mrs Delaney, while this was going on?

CATHY

I held my hand over his mouth to stop him screaming.

So you, as a mother, on the night before his birthday, were witness to the death struggle of your own son?

CATHY

Yes.

All things considered, do you think it's fair, what you did to your children?

CATHY

It's horrific.

At the time of the events, you weren't married.

CATHY

No.

Cathy Delaney, you've been writing letters, a great quantity . . . more than a hundred and fifty pages you've written?

CATHY

Yes.

After the events, you described Mr Delaney as 'a beast'.

CATHY

'God, I hate him! When that monster comes near me, I get the creeps. The things he committed on me are too filthy for words. I was abused, I was humiliated . . . '

He tied you up with shoelaces and raped you anally. He told you, 'You should be used to it, you had an affair with a homo.' And then, on his birthday, you wrote to your father and stepmother . . .

CATHY

'Today is that bastard's birthday. Things started going downhill for me the day he was born.'

You write that from jail on the tenth of May 1999, two months after the events.

CATHY

Yes.

. . . and then two years later, you marry him? How can you explain that?

CATHY

Because I love him.

Because you love him.

MICHAEL

We loved each other.

So, Mrs Delaney, why did you write things like that right after the events?

CATHY

That's how I felt.

That's how you felt . . . and then, after the events, in jail, then you got married? Just to get rid of any possible misunderstanding, here's my next question: Mrs Delaney, are you pregnant again at this point, or aren't you?

CATHY

No, sir, I'm not.

Is there anything you wish to add?

CATHY

It's the medication I'm on. I had a ph . . . a phantom pregnancy, too.

Michael stands up to say this, and for Cathy's following line:

MICHAEL

I want to say that I'm very sorry about what I did to my children. And that I miss them very much. And I would also ask my wife to forgive me for all the things I did to her.

CATHY

I would like to say that I miss my children very much, and that I'm very sorry about everything that happened, and that I also wish I could turn the clock back.

Good. Sit down. Mrs Delaney, were you strict with Matthew?

CATHY

Yes, I got angry with him a lot and I hit him quite often . . . because I was stressed by all the things Michael did to me.

**So you were stressed by all the things Michael did to
you, and your child, Matthew, had to bear the brunt?**

CATHY

Yes.

**So it's because you hadn't enough courage to stop
Mr Delaney that you made that little boy suffer. You
smacked him for the slightest thing. The child was
running around covered in bruises. Punching him in
the face, pushing him down the stairs, taping his
mouth shut. And when he was finicky with his food,
making him eat with a ladle. That boy never had a life,
did he, Mrs Delaney?**

**You did an aptitude test once, when you applied for a
job as a general domestic. What was that all about,
Mrs Delaney?**

CATHY

The job was cleaning. You have to do exams for everything
these days.

But you failed.

CATHY

I failed, but I've no reason . . . no idea why. I mean, what's so
hard about wringing a mop out? Then the police report says our
house is filthy. No, 'The house made a disorderly impression,'
that's how they put it. I said, 'Listen, if you don't have a
licence you can't drive. You lot're expecting me to scrub my
whole house down, when you won't even give me a certificate
to work as a cleaner!'

**The report also said it was 'a gloomy house' and that
it had a 'dismal atmosphere'.**

CATHY

I painted the light bulbs black. I love black. I shut the curtains
most of the time too. Day as well as night.

Whole days in the dark, Mr Delaney . . .

MICHAEL

So? We like it that way. It's a matter of taste, isn't it?

There were problems with the neighbours too?

MICHAEL

What's she been saying? We don't interfere with her shitey
wallpaper or those feathers in a flower vase in her living room,
do we? Now that is daft: why bird's feathers in a flower vase?
You wouldn't stick flowers up a bird's arse, would you?

CATHY

Her next door thinks I'm a witch, cos I always sit in the dark.

MICHAEL

I told her: 'When it gets too dark, we open the fridge door.'

CATHY

But then I think: 'Your kitchen's strip-lit like a chip shop! All
that light must give you a sore head.' If you don't put her in her
place, she'll just go on and on. She moans about everything.

They mentioned your music too.

CATHY

She complains about my music being too loud, but I'm sure
she wouldn't complain about other music. Does she expect me
to listen to the stuff she likes? Julio Iglesias? Julio Iglesias, she'd
sing along with that. She moans about everything. Said she
was bothered by our noisy arguments. So I told her: 'Don't
be stupid. Do you think we can argue *silently*?' Well, that shut
her up.

MICHAEL

She's single. If I was single, I wouldn't have arguments either.

**It wasn't just arguments, I hear. Wasn't there a
refrigerator thrown out of the window, Mr Delaney?**

MICHAEL

A what?

A refrigerator. A fridge.

MICHAEL

Well, the person who says that obviously can't tell the difference between a fridge and a telly! Imagine what their home's like! 'Anything good on the fridge tonight, dear?'

CATHY

From time to time he needs to throw something. It calms him down, makes him feel better.

It calms him down, makes him feel better.

MICHAEL

But she doesn't understand that. She's straight on the phone, cos our noise is disturbing her again. I'd *prefer* a television to fall to the ground without making all that racket, you know, but I can't help it, that's the way it is. You drop something, it smashes, it makes a noise. *Sorry!* Does she want us to live down a mine or something?

CATHY

She's jealous, of course, of us having two or three TVs, so that we can smash the odd one and let off steam. Why doesn't she just buy herself a few more tellies, then she can smash one herself from time to time!

It's jealousy, then, pure and simple?

MICHAEL

Yes, that's right, jealousy, that's what it is.

CATHY

That's it, that's the exact word!

MICHAEL

It's because we're on benefits. She thinks we shouldn't have three TVs or five stereos. As if being on the social means you have to live like a beggar. Anyway, she can go and ask for a TV too. She should go on the social, that's what it's there for! But she wouldn't dream of it, of course. She hates her job at the

factory, but she'd rather do it than make a claim. She's just
moaning cos she's too stuck up to claim the social.

CATHY

And guess what? She had the nerve to say to me: 'But Cathy,
surely you can only watch one television at a time?' I was like,
'What do you mean, you can only watch one telly at a time?
Have you never been to Comet? Well then!'

**I hear your baby used to cry for extended periods – for
'nights on end'.**

MICHAEL

Babies do that.

CATHY

A crybaby, that's the saying.

MICHAEL

That's what I told her. I said: 'To give you a good night's sleep
we have to slit the child's throat?' Then she started on about
something else, complaining about us having our telly on at
night. Well, sometimes two tellies. But my wife and I think it's
cosy, knowing the TV is playing downstairs while you're
sleeping. When I was a kid, I used to feel nice and cosy
hearing my folks talking downstairs when I was in my bed.
Because afterwards, when I lived in a home, there you didn't
have any of those sounds. There it was only silence.

CATHY

'My darling Moo, Here I am again with a letter. I managed to
get a stamp at last. Honey, I think of you all the time and
wonder how you're doing there, hoping you're not in too much
pain. I miss you so much, and especially now, because you're
so far away. My heart hurts terribly, it's just breaking for you.
I wish we were together. I wish our whole wee family could be
together again, because I miss all of you so much I can hardly
bear it. It's just unbearable. But still, we'll have to fight on for
the rest of our lives, and learn to live with it. Your darling, Coo.'

Was she asleep, or was she crying, or . . . ?

MICHAEL

No, she was awake.

She was awake, but she wasn't doing anything?

MICHAEL

No, sir.

She wasn't getting on your nerves?

MICHAEL

No.

She was quiet, just looking around?

MICHAEL

Yes.

Your three-month-old baby was lying peacefully in her bed, smiling?

MICHAEL

That's right.

That's right. The baby was lying smiling in her bed, you picked her up . . . and then you did what?

MICHAEL

I laid her on the bed, beside my wife.

On the bed, beside your wife . . . and then?

MICHAEL

I pushed her head into the mattress for a few seconds.

Into the mattress for a few seconds. Pushed her face into the mattress?

MICHAEL

Yes.

Why?

MICHAEL

To suffocate her.

To suffocate her. So at that moment, Mr Delaney, you wanted to end it, end her life?

Michael nods.

Yes. Why? Were you beginning to carry out a plan? 'All four of us were to die'?

MICHAEL

No.

Why did you want Ellie dead?

MICHAEL

To put an end to it.

To put an end to it. You pushed her face into the mattress, and then?

MICHAEL

I stopped straight away, I couldn't do it.

You stopped because you couldn't do it. And what happened?

MICHAEL

Then I told my wife, Here, you . . . she had to do it.

You told Mrs Delaney she had to do it.

MICHAEL

Yes.

And what did she do?

MICHAEL

She took a pillow and put it over her, then she lay on top of it.

She put a pillow over her. Over who?

MICHAEL

Over Ellie.

Over Ellie. And then?

MICHAEL

She lay on top of it.

And then she lay on top of Ellie? Did she say, 'OK, I'll help you do it'?

MICHAEL

No.

She did it, without a word?

MICHAEL

She was crying.

She was crying, but she lay down on top of Ellie?

MICHAEL

Yes, sir.

Did she know, at that moment, what she was doing to Ellie . . . what would be the consequence of lying on top of her?

MICHAEL

I suppose so.

How long did she stay like that, on top of Ellie?

MICHAEL

About fifteen minutes.

Fifteen minutes. Was Ellie lying face down at this point?

MICHAEL

That . . . I can't remember.

In any case, either there was a pillow under Ellie, or there was one between Cathy and Ellie. So it's either: pillow/Ellie/Cathy, or Ellie/pillow/Cathy. Mr Delaney?

MICHAEL

First Ellie, then pillow, and on top of that my wife.

You knew what you were doing? You knew what it meant to lie on a baby for fifteen minutes? You knew Ellie wouldn't survive? Mr Delaney? Did you know that?

MICHAEL

Yes.

You didn't want Ellie to survive, did you?

MICHAEL

I didn't realise what was happening.

You didn't realise what was happening? But afterwards you stated to the police that 'it needed ending'. Didn't you, Mr Delaney?

MICHAEL

Yes, and then I told her she was a child murderer!

Mrs Delaney, is that how it happened?

CATHY

I can't remember.

You can't remember. What did happen, according to you?

CATHY

I don't know, sir.

You don't notice her?

CATHY

No: I . . . don't . . . know . . . sir.

So you don't know?

CATHY

No.

What strikes me as strange is . . . *why* don't you remember?

CATHY

He hit me about the head.

He hit you. When did he hit you?

CATHY

Must have been Thursday. Sometime on Thursday.

Severe beatings, I believe?

CATHY

Yes, pretty bad.

What did Mr Delaney do to you?

CATHY

He slapped me in the face, burnt me with a cigarette. And he carved my legs with a razor and wrote the letter M in my pubic hair.

And he cut your hair off too?

CATHY

And then he said, 'Let's see if you feel like a woman now.'

Is that true, Mr Delaney?

MICHAEL

Yes.

And why did you do all that?

MICHAEL

I don't know.

'I don't know.' You don't know! That's always the
easiest answer, isn't it? You wanted to humilate her,
that's what you said at the time. You were jealous,
weren't you, because you thought she was having an
affair with a Mark Hurst? And so you wrote an M in
her pubic hair. Is that so?

MICHAEL

It's possible.

What's possible?

MICHAEL

That I might have said that. It's possible I might have said
that.

CATHY

It's possible, he might have said that.

MICHAEL

'My darling, it may be hard, sweetheart, but we really must
talk about the gravestones and a few sayings or poems to go on
them. I've already been over it with the prison social workers,
and they're going to give us some books so that we can choose
things from. But it's up to us to decide, to decide ourselves on a
saying or a poem. Sweetheart, I hope I'm going to see you soon,
cos I'm going crazy in here. Time goes so terribly fa . . . slow.
I love you, darling. Your sweetheart, Moo.'

You were forced to swallow tablets?

CATHY

And drink beer.

And drink beer.

CATHY

And he also made me order a bottle of champagne.

Right. On that Thursday you were drinking
champagne. Did you have something to celebrate?

MICHAEL

We didn't touch it. It was spilt, it fell over.

Mrs Delaney, you made a statement: 'Afterwards we drank champagne.' You had to go downstairs to get it, and . . . and what did Mr Delaney make you say? You had to explain: 'We have something to celebrate . . . '

CATHY

I don't know any more.

You say now, Mrs Delaney, 'I don't know any more, I was out cold, I wasn't aware of what was happening . . . '

CATHY

Yes.

. . . 'That Thursday night,' you told the officers, 'I held my wee girl to my chest and kept her there until I was sure she was no longer alive. My husband agreed to it.'

CATHY

That's what Michael told me I'd done.

So the three of you stayed another two days in that hotel room with your daughter's body lying there? Didn't Matthew ask about his sister?

CATHY

We told him she was asleep, that she was ill.

But didn't he want to play with her? I can imagine that a boy of seven would like to play with his sister?

CATHY

He wanted to go and see her once, but Michael just said, 'Leave it.' I could never hurt my children.

You could never hurt your children?

CATHY

No, sir.

**Ah . . . But two days after you had smothered his baby
sister, on the night before his birthday, you wrapped a
blanket around the head of a seven-year-old boy. And
you don't call that hurting your children?**

CATHY

I didn't wrap it around his head. I put it over his head.

You wrapped it around his head, that's what you said.

CATHY

No.

**You said it yourself: 'He put up quite a struggle. He
called out, "Mummy, Mummy, don't hurt me, I don't
want to die . . . " '**

Silence.

And then, what else happened that night?

CATHY

I went downstairs for a packet of cigarettes, and then I lay on
the bed . . . I woke up. I heard noises in the street outside –
traffic, singing – and then I thought: it's true, I'm not at home,
we're in a hotel room.

My neck was hurting, cos we'd wrapped Ellie's body in a
pillowcase, and I just can't stand to lay my head on a pillow
without a pillowcase – definitely not in a hotel. You never
know who's been lying on that pillow, you never know what
other folk have been doing in that bed. People do the weirdest
things in hotel rooms, and you'd never know about it. And so
I'd been sleeping without a pillow. It was only when I felt my
stiff neck that I remembered why we were there.

Michael was lying with his back to me, and Matthew was asleep
as well, the wee lamb. I looked at him for a minute, then I
thought, 'This is it.' I put the blanket over his head, to suffocate
him. But he woke up and started to fight me off. If I'd been
stronger at that moment, harder, it would have been over there

and then. But he struggled free. He cried, 'Mummy, Mummy, don't hurt me, I don't want to die.' His eyes were like a cow's. He looked at me like a cow going past in a truck. 'I don't want to die.' Meanwhile, Michael had woken up. 'What the hell are you doing? Let me get some sleep!' He can't stand being woken up. I cuddled the boy, and told him I was sorry.

Then I went downstairs to get some fags from the machine. Funnily enough, I nearly put my coins in the condom machine. My mind was on other things, I suppose. There was a drunk in the lobby who saw me go to the condom machine with all those coins and said: 'Hey, missus, it's well seen you don't want any kids!' Then I realised my mistake, so I straightened up and went to the cigarette machine. Like I said, my mind was on other things.

Then when I got back to the room and sat down on the edge of the bed with my ciggy, I saw the boy looking at me. Still with those cow's eyes. I'd never be able to make it up to him, I knew it: he'd never forget what I'd tried to do. I also knew he wouldn't sleep any more that night, or at least, he'd try not to sleep: because he didn't trust me any more. And while he was looking at me like that and I was sitting there, smoking, I was reminded of myself.

My father always used to light a cigarette just after he had come inside me. And I'd look at him, lying on his back, slowly blowing smoke at the ceiling. Smoking is a form of sighing. I was twelve when I started smoking, and I smoked my first cigarettes exactly like my dad did. I blew the smoke out just like him.

'If our Matthew gets a bit older, he'll end up a smoker too.' That's what I was thinking then.

MICHAEL
What were we supposed to do? Every parent wants the best for their kid. When I was a wee boy, my mother used to slap me in the face, and straight after she'd say, 'That's cos I love you.' I'm telling you, every parent wants the best for their kid.

Yes, our house was filthy. We never bothered to clean. Why clean the place up if it's going to get filthy again the next day? Sometimes we were stoned when we went to school to pick up the boy. One time we were so stoned we almost took the wrong kid home with us. Mind you, he did look like our Matthew, but if we'd been straight we wouldn't have made that mistake.

I used to beat his mother and fuck her arse while he sat and played in the corner with some old clothes. We never got him any proper toys. We told him: 'Santa Claus doesn't come for bad kids.'

What were we supposed to do? It wouldn't have lasted much longer. I was giving it a year, two at most, before someone was on to us. Child welfare would have interfered: taken our kids away and put them in a home. 'For their own good.' Well, they put me in a home, 'for my own good', and I came out with a criminal record as long as your arm. It did me a *lot* of good, that place did!

There aren't many things I know for sure, but one thing I do know is: no one will ever put any of my kids in a home. Over my dead body.

What were we supposed to do? We wiped out our kids. Don't tell me we didn't want the best for them.

Then you went to fetch cigarettes.

CATHY

And then Michael came and sat next to me on the bed, and he stroked my face and said he was sorry.

Right. That night, did you discuss what to do next?

CATHY

No.

Mr Delaney?

MICHAEL

No, sir.

Then when did you decide on the next move?

MICHAEL

On Friday.

On Friday. Because, as a matter of fact, Mr Delaney, you stated, 'Yes, Cathy tried to choke him with a blanket and sheet, and Matthew put up quite a struggle.'

MICHAEL

Yes.

So that's not 'putting a blanket over his head', is it? You intended to suffocate him, didn't you?

MICHAEL

Yes, sir.

And what more did Mrs Delaney propose to do, after she had stopped holding the blanket over Matthew's head?

MICHAEL

Nothing. We just sat side by side. We didn't say a word after that.

You didn't say a word after that. But you did make other plans to kill him, didn't you? You wanted to kill Matthew. You must have thought up another idea?

MICHAEL

Yes, on Friday . . .

CATHY

. . . we wanted to electrocute him.

You wanted to electrocute him.

CATHY

I was supposed to give him a bath and then drop a live wire in the water. But we never went through with it.

And the idea of electrocution, whose was it?

CATHY

Mine.

It was your idea. And when did this come to you?

CATHY

On Friday.

On Friday?

CATHY

Yes, sir.

So one way or another, Matthew had to die?

CATHY

Yes.

Mr Delaney?

MICHAEL

Yes.

**You were going to electrocute him. Mrs Delaney . . .
I put it to you that you're quite a cool and calculating
woman. First you try to jump on him, put a blanket
and a sheet over his head, and the next day you plan
to electrocute him. Where did you get the idea of
electrocution?**

CATHY

I don't remember, sir.

**You don't remember. The easiest answer, of course.
That plan . . . what steps did you take to carry it out?**

CATHY

We never carried it out.

But you did prepare certain things, didn't you?

CATHY

Eh, no . . .

No?!

CATHY

No.

**How did you think you were going to electrocute
anyone without electricity and without a live wire?**

CATHY

We cut a wire loose.

**There you are: preparation. Can you confirm that, Mr
Delaney?**

MICHAEL

Yes, sir.

**The boy had a stomach ache. I don't suppose it was
due to overeating. He didn't get much to eat, did he, in
those days leading up to the events? I noticed that you
didn't have any breakfast either on Saturday morning?**

CATHY

No.

**And you said, 'Come here with your sore tummy,
come and lie on my lap,' and there he was, lying with
his head on your lap. And then what happened?**

CATHY

Then Michael sat beside me on the bed and took up
Matthew's legs and put them over his own knees.

Lifted his legs. Can you confirm that, Mr Delaney?

MICHAEL

Yes, that's right.

**So you took his legs and what happened then? What
did you do next, Mr Delaney?**

MICHAEL

I took a pair of scissors that were lying behind me.

They were lying ready for you?

CATHY

On the bedside table.

On the bedside table.

CATHY

Behind him.

Behind him.

MICHAEL

On the bedside table.

On the bedside table. But they were lying ready for you there? So you knew clearly at that moment what you were going to do to Matthew? You knew he had to die?

CATHY

Yes.

Mr Delaney?

MICHAEL

Yes, sir.

So was that the plan, Mrs Delaney? 'You take hold of his legs and then we kill him'?

CATHY

Yes.

Mr Delaney?

MICHAEL

That's right.

What did you do then?

MICHAEL

I stabbed those scissors into his back.

You stabbed those scissors into his back. And what did you do, Mrs Delaney, while this was going on?

CATHY

I held my hand over his mouth to stop him screaming.

You held your hand over his mouth to stop him screaming?

CATHY

Yes, and then I . . .

You were also holding his hand, weren't you?

CATHY

Yes, he was squeezing my hand. Then he let go.

Then he let go. That is, you, his mother, were there from the beginning to the very end of the boy's death struggle . . . on the night before his birthday.

CATHY

Yes.

You felt his hand go slack?

CATHY

And he was also pressing on my thigh, right where I had a burn.

He was pressing on your thigh . . .

CATHY

Yes, where I had a burn.

And what did you do then, Mr Delaney?

MICHAEL

I got up and went to the bathroom and slit my wrists.

Then you . . . Does that mean you put Matthew down on the floor before you got up?

MICHAEL

Yes, sir.

Yes, sir.

MICHAEL

And we covered him with a blanket.

**You covered him with a blanket . . . so you wouldn't
have to see him?**

MICHAEL

Yes.

**And then you went to the bathroom . . . meaning to slit
your wrists. And did you?**

MICHAEL

Yes.

**Well, hardly, or you wouldn't be sitting there now,
would you? What did you do then, Mrs Delaney?**

CATHY

I never meant to kill myself.

So why did you say that to the police?

CATHY

To help Michael.

To help Michael?

CATHY

To back him up, in his words.

But you did try to kill yourself, didn't you?

CATHY

I asked Michael to slit my wrists.

Hadn't you tried to do it yourself first?

CATHY

Yes, sir, with a beer can.

With a beer can . . .

CATHY

Yes.

You tried to slit your wrists?

CATHY

Yes.

And you found you couldn't?

CATHY

That's right.

And then, what did you do? You asked him to do it?

CATHY

Yes, I asked him.

Mr Delaney, what did you do next?

MICHAEL

She was begging me.

She was begging you. So what did you do?

MICHAEL

I slit her wrists.

Slit her wrists.

MICHAEL

With a razor.

You used that razor to cut her wrists. You were back in the bathroom, I presume?

MICHAEL

Yes.

Yes. And did you try to do anything else to yourself?

MICHAEL
I tried to stick those scissors into my back . . . belly.

You tried to stick those scissors into your belly.

MICHAEL
Yes.

Your statement said, 'I wanted to cut myself away.'

MICHAEL
Yes.

But you didn't do it? You were too much of a coward?

MICHAEL
I couldn't do it.

What's that?

MICHAEL
I couldn't do it.

You couldn't do it? But you could do it to Matthew, couldn't you? With the same scissors? The scissors that were still covered in your son's blood, you were too much of a coward to stab yourself with them?

CATHY
And I could still feel Matthew.

You could still see Matthew?

CATHY
No, I could still *feel* Matthew.

Oh, you could still feel Matthew?

CATHY
Yes. His leg was lying on mine.

Oh, I see, his leg was lying on yours . . . All things considered, do you think it's fair what you did to your children?

CATHY

It's horrific.

You two made a mess of your lives, wouldn't you agree? You both rejected all the chances society gave you. When people offered you help, you wouldn't take it, you wouldn't take anything except for the money. And who were the victims?

CATHY

The children.

Matthew and Ellie.

CATHY

Matthew and Ellie.

They had found each other. Their lives had drifted towards each other, become entwined, interwoven, knotted, soldered, fused, hammered and beaten together – and it was clear that only a considerable blow would ever break their bond.

Of course, each had seen their life go down the drain. It was at the bottom of the sewer, you might say, that they rolled together: rolled together in a little heap. But together is what they were. And Cathy Delaney repeatedly told the judge, in answer to every question, 'I loved him, I followed him in everything he did.'

'Love is blind,' says someone, but it sounds like he says it with a touch of envy. 'Love is blind, and the guide dog's always getting lost.'

What does the psychiatrist say, who was called to testify, to disclose the twists and warps of their minds

to the lawyers and the press. What does he say? Are
they declared fully accountable? Yes, they are clearly
of normal intelligence; just look at those two faces.
'They have normal brains and their brains function
normally.'

The psychiatrist mentions a sociopathic personality,
but brushes aside any alleged paranoid or schizotypal
traits: not material. 'No serious psychiatric disorder
can be found in the minds of these two. They are
completely normal.'

Did you have financial difficulties, Mr Delaney?

MICHAEL

If we'd been loaded, we wouldn't have gone on the social,
would we?

CATHY

We're always slagged off for having five stereos, but no one
ever mentions they aren't paid for yet.

MICHAEL

Those things don't belong to you until you've paid for them in
full.

CATHY

Really, we had nothing.

MICHAEL

That's right, we hadn't paid for anything, so how could we
have anything? Really, you can't throw away stuff you don't
even own yet.

That doesn't demonstrate very good money
management, does it, Mrs Delaney?

CATHY

We couldn't manage money! We're smart enough to let the
social pay our bills, you know.

MICHAEL

They even sent us meals.

CATHY

Hot meals.

MICHAEL

And when we weren't in, they left the food on the doorstep.
Couldn't manage money?!

CATHY

When we didn't like what they brought, we just left it there. It
was good enough for the cats.

**Ah, what an attitude! What society offers isn't good
enough for you then? Fussy about food as well?**

MICHAEL

I don't like fish and I'm not going to like it any better just cos
I was given it free.

CATHY

Those meals were disgusting sometimes. I'd rather eat dirt.

MICHAEL

But because you get it for free, you're supposed to be grateful.

Your home must have been quite a mess.

CATHY

I suppose it was.

**And then a social worker came to see you, after you'd
had the debt collectors knocking at your door.**

CATHY

She asked us if we'd heard of Lidl. But I told her, I said, 'Lidl
isn't for the likes of us. Because do you know who shops at
Lidl? Rich penny-pinchers. They've got everything already and
they want even more. They're the ones who shop at Lidl, not
poor people.'

It must have been hard on you, Mrs Delaney.

CATHY

Do you know they don't use price labels? The cashiers just ring up whatever they like. They claim to know all the prices by heart, but who says they really do? Who says they know each and every price by heart? Does anyone ever check them? I think they just ring up what they want. They see a tin of beans and go, 'Oh, that'll be . . . whatever.'

MICHAEL

Did you know that Lidl is owned by two brothers and they're in the top three richest people on earth? Now how do you think they managed that? Not by ringing up the right prices every time!

The people who ring up prices at Lidl, Mr Delaney, are people who are willing to work for a living.

MICHAEL

They always say, 'Money isn't everything,' but if you –

CATHY

– if you don't have any money, they come and tell you you've got to go and work so that you can get some! Where's the logic in that?

MICHAEL

It's the system.

The system? What do you mean by that?

MICHAEL

Nothing. I suppose we'd be better off dead? Maybe that would've been better. We wouldn't be a problem to you then.

Arguments . . . fights . . . drinking sessions . . . never making ends meet, buying all kinds of fripperies, roaming the streets, living on benefits. You let society help you with money all right. Your attitude is that you don't give a damn about . . . the whole world, the whole of society.

CATHY

Right.

You agree then?

CATHY

Yes.

You don't give a damn, either of you, do you? You couldn't care less about other people, about society?

CATHY

Yes.

But you do want society to help you with money?

CATHY

That's right.

Is that right, Mr Delaney?

MICHAEL

Yes.

Society's good enough for that, is it?

MICHAEL

Yes, sir.

Social parasites. Would you agree with that description?

CATHY

Sure.

Mr Delaney?

MICHAEL

That's it.

So you want to be given everything, but you'll give nothing back, and you refuse to stick to the rules. The only rules you live by are your own. You had cars, too, now and again, didn't you?

MICHAEL

I don't have a driving licence.

No, you don't, but did you have cars? Did you ever drive cars?

MICHAEL

Yes.

But you didn't have a licence.

MICHAEL

No.

And those cars you drove, were they registered?

MICHAEL

No.

And were they insured?

MICHAEL

No. You'd have to be pretty thick to take out insurance for a car that isn't even registered.

Seven years away from Aalst.

MICHAEL

I'm starting to feel like I'm here for a traffic offence!

Why did you go back?

You took a pair of scissors and a razor. Why did you take a pair of scissors and a razor?

They were after you. Who was after you?

You took them for self-defence.

What gang?

For two nights you slept in the car, then on Tuesday night you didn't sleep, you drove all night, till you ended up in Aalst.

Where exactly did you end up? Yes, at a hotel. Which hotel exactly? When was this?

At four thirty in the morning.

And how much did you pay for a room in that hotel?

Including breakfast?

Did you have breakfast?

No?! Even though you were entitled to breakfast, you had paid for breakfast, you didn't have any breakfast?

You couldn't be bothered. But you could be bothered to barricade the door of your room?

You sent out for some chips. And how about Ellie? She couldn't eat chips. You made her some formula. Did you heat it for her? In a bucket of warm water in the room. You didn't think of asking the staff to warm it for you? Or you didn't want to?

You didn't think of it. And then you barricaded the door? Why did you barricade the door?

There was nothing to go out for. So you just stayed in.

CATHY

I wanted to be with Michael.

How or where or what you didn't know, but you knew it had to finish. It had to end.

MICHAEL

Yes.

Mrs Delaney, you've had brushes with the law before, haven't you? In 1992, you took some clothes and jewellery, and you damaged the clothes, you tore them when you ripped off the security tags. They caught you red-handed.

CATHY

Well, eh . . . I walked out of the shop . . . eh, yes, with some
jewellery and clothes. But no one asked me for a receipt. Who
says I stole them?

The tags had been ripped out!

CATHY

Yes, they were, but, eh . . . I mean . . . they could have asked
me whether I had a receipt, couldn't they? I mean . . . they
never even bothered to ask me . . .

**They had been following you around the shop. They
saw you do it!**

CATHY

That's exactly what I mean, they jumped to conclusions. What
I mean is, they never asked me how it had happened, I mean,
eh . . . no one asked me whether those were things I was
planning on paying for or not. Things I might have been *happy*
to pay for. But no, they never asked me anything, they put two
and two together, and jumped to conclusions, and that was it.

**Just a moment: they caught you outside the shop,
didn't they?**

CATHY

Yes, sir.

With items you hadn't paid for?

CATHY

Yes.

**Yes. Were you going to wear those clothes and jewellery
or did you intend to sell them?**

CATHY

They were just things I was going to wear. For personal use.
They were things for women. You know, *women's* things.
Dresses, and earrings, and accessories and not, like, a car radio
or something! Not like a camera! Not the kind of thing you
would plan to sell or anything.

You can sell clothes, can't you?

CATHY

Yes, in theory, but it's a product that's very hard to sell.

Have you tried?

CATHY

I tried once. It was a little black dress. I'd lost weight and so
I asked a friend, 'Would you like to buy this off me?' She said,
'OK, I'll buy it,' but she never did. In fact, she never mentioned
it again.

**I get the impression that, if I were to let you walk out
of here, you would just carry on as before.**

CATHY

I'm telling you, sir, you lot, you only see one side of the
problem. But you don't see the whole picture. Crime isn't
something you do for fun, you know. Not unless, eh . . . not
unless you're sick in the head.

**Mrs Delaney, do you want to spend the rest of your
life in prison?**

CATHY

No, sir, I don't. Maybe, eh . . . maybe I should leave the
country?

To go and steal abroad?

CATHY

Well, I suppose so, I might not have a choice, you know. As if
you care, or those social workers . . . You don't give a damn.

**You don't seem to realise you've already *had* your last
chance!**

CATHY

Well, sir, perhaps I'd better end it. Is that what you want? It
would be much easier, wouldn't it? So much better. All right:
just tell me, and I'll do it. I'll hang myself, so you're rid of me.

No one's interested anyway, no one cares. I'll be out of the way then. Just let me know and you'll never have to set eyes on me again. I'll slit my wrists. Maybe then I'll fit into your system.

You don't seem to show any remorse, do you, Mrs Delaney?

CATHY

Yes, I do. My heart is wide open for my children.

What do you mean by that?

CATHY

I don't know.

Don't you think you should apologise?

CATHY

Who to?

To the people you hurt.

CATHY

I've been hurt too! It's strange, isn't it, sir, we were never taught anything about 'life' at school. Never. All you got was: 'What's the capital of Peru?'

MICHAEL

This whole thing is a nightmare for us.

CATHY

Our kids were the most precious things we had.

MICHAEL

We wanted to wipe out our problems . . .

CATHY

You don't seem to understand that! We . . . had . . . problems.

MICHAEL

. . . And we thought it would be better to wipe out the whole family. It isn't fair, sir: there are people who *make* a baby to save their marriage, no one objects to that, that's allowed, you can *have* kids for any purpose you like. But when someone wipes out their kids to finally get *out* of the misery, they're hauled up before the courts! Everyone picks on us.

The lights dim.

MICHAEL

How was it?

CATHY

It was perfect. Very convincing. That's five years off your sentence, I'm sure.

MICHAEL

Your turn!

CATHY

I can't say the same thing, of course, that wouldn't work.

MICHAEL

Something with a saying in it would be good. To strike a chord. Good to use something that appeals to people.

CATHY

A child without a mother is like a vase without flowers.

MICHAEL

No, that's a bit much. You shouldn't make it too difficult, Coo. Remember, some of those folk aren't educated.

CATHY

Regrets always come too late.

MICHAEL

Can't you think of anything else? You sound as if you're reading from a proverb-a-day calendar.

CATHY

I wish I could turn the clock back.

MICHAEL

Cathy Delaney, is there anything you wish to add?

CATHY

I would like to say that I miss my children very much and that I'm very sorry about what happened. And that I wish I could turn the clock back, because what we did was not exactly brilliant.

Fade to black.